For Huck –
sharing stories –

Barry Lopez

RIVER NOTES

ALSO BY BARRY HOLSTUN LOPEZ

Non-fiction
Of Wolves and Men, 1978

Fiction
Desert Notes: Reflections in the Eye of a Raven, 1976
Giving Birth to Thunder, Sleeping with His Daughter, 1978

RIVER NOTES

The Dance of Herons

Barry Holstun Lopez

Andrews and McMeel, Inc.
A Universal Press Syndicate Company
Kansas City

Library of Congress Cataloging in Publication Data

Lopez, Barry Holstun, 1945-
   River notes.

   I. Title.
PZ4.L86356Ri   [PS3562.067]   813'.5'4   79-17192
ISBN 0-8362-6106-2

for Sandy

CONTENTS

INTRODUCTION

I am exhausted. I have been standing here for days watching the ocean curl against the beach, and have sunk very gradually over all these hours to the sand where I lie now, worn out with the waiting. At certain moments, early in the morning most often, before sunrise, I have known exactly what I was watching the water for—but at this hour there is no light, it is hard to see, and so the moment passes without examination.

I do not consider this cruel, nor am I discouraged. I have been here too long.

In the predawn hours I watch the sky, the small distant suns, as winter comes on, of Orion and Canis Major shining above the southern horizon. I can easily imagine a planet among them on the surface of which someone is standing alone in a clearing trying to teach himself to whistle, and is being watched by large birds that look like herons. (I reach out and begin to dig in the sand, feeling for substance, for stones in the earth to hold onto: I might suddenly lose my own weight, be blown away like a duck's breast feather in the slight breeze that now tunnels in my hair.)

I stand back up, resume the watch. I know what I'm looking for. I wait.

I do not know what to do with the weariness, with the exhaustion. I confess to self-delusion. I've imagined myself walking away at times, as though bored or defeated, but contriving to leave enough of myself behind to observe any sign, the slightest change. I would seem to an observer to be absorbed in a game of string figures between my fingers, inattentive, when in fact I would be alert to the heartbeats of fish moving beyond the surf. But these ruses only added to the weariness and seemed, in the end, irreverent.

I have been here, I think, for years. I have spent nights with my palms flat on the sand, tracing the grains for hours like braille until I had the pattern precisely, could go anywhere—the coast of Africa—and recreate the same strip of beach, down to the very sound of the water on sea pebbles out of the sound of my gut that has been empty for years; to the welling of the wind by vibrating the muscles of my thighs. Replications. I could make you believe you heard sandpipers walking in the darkness at the edge of a spent wave, or a sound that would make you cry at the thought of what had slipped through your fingers. When tides and the wind and the scurrying of creatures rearrange these interminable grains of sand so that I must learn this surface all over again through the palms of my hands, I do. This is one of my confidences.

I have spent much of my time simply walking.

Once I concentrated very hard on moving soundlessly down the beach. I anticipated individual grains of sand losing their grip and tumbling into depressions, and I moved at that moment so my footfalls were masked. I imagined myself in between these steps as silent as stone stairs, but poised, like the heron hunting. In this way I eventually became unknown even to myself (looking somewhere out to sea for a flight of terns to pass). I could then examine myself as though I were an empty abalone shell, held up in my own hands, held up to the wind to see what sort of noise I would make. I knew the sound—the sound of fish dreaming, twilight in a still pool downstream of rocks in a mountain river.

I dreamed I was a salmon, listening to the noise of water in my dreaming, and in this way returned, moving in the cool evening air wrapped in a camouflage of sound down the beach (over a wide floor of gray-streaked Carrara marble, naked) down the beach (my skin taut, each muscle enunciated as smooth and dense beneath the skin as marble) as silent as snowing.

There are birds here.

I hold in my heart an absolute sorrow for birds, a sorrow so deep that at the first light of day when I shiver like reeds clattering in a fall wind I do not know whether it is from the cold or from this sorrow, whether I am even capable of feeling such kindness. I believe yes, I am.

One rainy winter dawn I stood beneath gray clouds with my arms upstretched, dripping in my light cotton clothes in the familiar ritual, staring at the sand at my feet, about to form a prayer, when I felt birds alight. I felt first the flutter of golden plovers against my head, then black turnstones landing soft as butterflies on my arms, and red phalarope with their wild arctic visions, fighting the wind to land, prickling my shoulders with their needling grip. Their sudden windiness, the stiff brushing of wings, the foreign voices—murrelets alighting on my arms, blinking, blinking yellow eyes, sanderlings, whimbrels, and avocets jumping at my sides. Under them slowly, under heavy eider ducks, beneath the weight of their flapping pleading, I began to go down. As I came to my knees I could feel such anguish as must lie unuttered in the hearts of far-ranging birds, the weight of visions draped over their delicate bones.

Beneath the frantic, smothering wingbeats I recalled the birds of my childhood. I had stoned a robin. I thought the name given the kittiwake very funny. The afternoon of the day my mother died I lay on my bed wondering if I would get her small teakwood trunk with the beautiful brass fittings and its silver padlock. I coveted it in cold contradiction to my show of grief. Feeling someone watching I rolled over and through the window saw sparrows staring at me all explode like buckshot after our eyes met and were gone.

When I awoke the sky had cleared. In the damp sea air I could smell cedar pollen. I washed in a freshwater pool where a river broke out of the shore trees, ran across the beach, and buried itself in the breakers. I took talum roots at the pool's edge and crushed them against the native stone to make a kind of soap and began to wash. I washed the ashes of last night's fire from my hands and washed away a fear of darkness I was now heir to, sleeping alone and exposed on the broad beach. I moved out deeper into the stream, working up a lather in the cold water, scrubbing until my skin shouted with the cold and the rubbing, moving like a man who could dance hard and well alone.

I began each day like this, as though it were the last. I know the last days will be here, where the sun runs into the ocean, and that I will see in a movement of sea birds and hear in the sound of water beating against the earth what I now only imagine, that the ocean has a sadness beyond even the sadness of birds, that in the running into it of rivers is the weeping of the earth for what is lost.

By evening, when confirmation of these thoughts seems again withheld, I think of going back upriver, or up some other river than this one, to begin again.

I will tell you something. It is to the thought of the river's banks that I most frequently return, their wordless emergence at a headwaters, the control they urge on the direction of the river, mile after mile, and their disappearance here on the beach as the river enters the ocean. It occurs to me that at the very end the river is suddenly abandoned, that just before it's finished the edges disappear completely, that in this moment a whole life is revealed.

It is possible I am wrong. It is impossible to speak with certainty about very much.

It will not rain for the rest of the day. Lie down here and sleep. When you awake you will feel the pull of warm winds and wish to be gone. I will be standing somewhere on the beach staring at the breakers or the pirouettes of sanderlings, meditating on the distant murmuring of whales; but I can as easily turn inland, go upriver, and begin again.

When you awake, if you follow the river into the trees I will be somewhere ahead or beyond, like a flight of crows. When you are suddenly overwhelmed with a compassion that staggers you and you begin to run along the bank, at a moment when your fingers brush the soft skin of a deer-head orchid and you see sun-drenched bears stretching in an open field like young men, you will know a loss of guile and that the journey has begun.

THE SEARCH FOR THE HERON

I see you on the far side of the river, standing at the edge of familiar shadows, before a terrified chorus of young alders on the bank. I do not think you know it is raining. You are oblivious to the *thuck* of drops rolling off the tube of your neck and the slope of your back. (Above, in the sweepy cedars, drops pool at the tips of leather needles, break away, are sheered by the breeze and, *thuck*, hit the hollow-boned, crimson-colored shoulders of the bird and fall swooning into the river.)

Perhaps you know it is raining. The intensity of your stare is then not oblivion, only an effort to spot between the rain splashes in the river (past your feet, so well-known, there beneath the hammered surface like twigs in the pebbles) the movement of trout.

I know: your way is to be inscrutable. When pressed you leave. This is no more unexpected or mysterious than that you give birth to shadows. Or silence. I watch from a distance. With respect. I think of standing beside you when you have died of your own brooding over the water—as shaken as I would be at the collapse of a cathedral, wincing deep inside as at the screech of an overloaded cart.

You carry attribution well, refusing to speak. With your warrior's feathers downsloped at the back of your head, those white sheaves formed like a shield overlaying your breast, your gray-blue cast, the dark tail feathers—do you wear wolves' tails about your ankles and dance in clearings in the woods when your blood is running? I wonder where you have fought warrior. Where!

You retreat beneath your cowl, spread wings, rise, drift upriver as silent as winter trees.

I follow you. You have caught me with your reticence. I will listen to whatever they say about you, what anyone who has seen you wishes to offer—and I will return to call across the river to you, to confirm or deny. If you will not speak I will have to consider making you up.

Your sigh, I am told, is like the sound of rain driven against tower bells. You smell like wild ginger. When you lift your foot from the river, water doesn't run off it to spoil the transparent surface of the shallows. The water hesitates to offend you. You stare down with that great yellow eye, I am told, like some prehistoric rattlesnake: that dangerous, that blinding in your strike, that hate-ridden. But (someone else has insisted) you really do smell like wild ginger, and snakes smell like cucumbers. A false lead.

Cottonwoods along the river, stained with your white excrement, are young enough to volunteer complaint about you. They have grown so fast and so high with such little effort that they can understand neither failure nor triumph. So they will say anything they think might be to their advantage. I, after a somewhat more difficult life, am aware that they will lie, and that lies serve in their way.

(It was one of these who told me you were without mercy and snakelike.) One of them said something about your fishy breath—vulgar talk, I know. But I heard it out. It is, after all, in

4

their branches where you have dreamed at night, as immobile as a piece of lumber left in their limbs, and considered your interior life. This idea attracts me. I know: this is not something to inquire into with impunity, but I did not start out on this to please you. And in spite of my impatience I am respectful.

One dream alone reveals your grief. The trees said you dreamed most often of the wind. You dreamed that you lived somewhere with the wind, with the wind rippling your feathers; and that children were born of this, that they are the movement of water in all the rivers. You wade, it is suggested, among your children, staring hard, pecking in that lightning way your life from the water that is your child; and sleeping in trees that do not hold you sacred.

I know why you appear so fierce and self-contained. I can imagine fear in the form of a frog in your beak screaming and you, undisturbed, cool. When you finally speak up, feigning ignorance with me won't do; enigmatic locutions, distracting stories of the origin of the universe—these will not do. I expect the wisdom of the desert out of you.

The cottonwoods also told me of a dance, that you dreamed of a dance: more than a hundred great blue herons riveted by the light of dawn, standing with wind-riffled feathers on broad slabs of speckled gray granite, river-washed bedrock, in that sharp, etching backlight, their sleek bills glinting, beginning to lift their feet from the thin sheet of water and to put them back down. The sound of the rhythmic splash, the delicate *kersplash* of hundreds of feet, came up in the sound of the river and so at first was lost; but the shards of water, caught blinding in the cutting light (now the voices, rising, a keening) began to form a mist in which appeared rainbows against the white soft breasts; and where drops of water dolloped like beads of mercury on the blue-gray feathers, small rainbows of light here, and in the eyes (as the voices, louder, gathering on one, high, trembling note) rainbows—the birds cradled in light shattered in rainbows everywhere, and with your great blue wings fanning that brilliant mist, open, utterly vulnerable and stunning, you urged them to begin to revolve in the light, stretching their wings, and you lay back your head and closed the steely eyes and from deep within your belly came the roar of a cataract, like the howling of wolves—that long moment of your mournful voice. The birds quieted, their voices quieted. The water quieted, it quieted, until there was only your quivering voice, the sound of the birth of rivers, tapering finally to silence, to the sound of dawn, the birds standing there full of grace. One or two feathers floating on the water.

I understand it is insensitive to inquire further, but you see now your silence becomes even more haunting.

I believe we will dance together someday. Before then will I have to have been a trout, bear scars from your stabbing misses and so have some deeper knowledge? Then will we dance? I cannot believe it is so far between knowing what must be done and doing it.

The cottonwoods, these too-young trees, said once, long ago, you had a premonition in a nightmare. An enormous owl arrived while you slept and took your daughter away, pinioned in his gray fists. You woke, bolt upright, in the middle of the night to find her there, undisturbed beside you. You aired your feathers, glared into the moon-stilled space over the water and went uneasily back to sleep. In the morning—your first glance—the limb was empty. You were young, you had also lost a wife, and you went down to the river and tore out your feathers and wept. The soundlessness of it was what you could not get over.

The cottonwoods said there was more, but I put up my hand, tired, on edge at the sound of my own voice asking questions. I went into the trees, wishing to cry, I thought, for what had been lost, feeling how little I knew, how anxious I was, how young.

The big maples, where you have slept since then—I resolved to ask them about your dreams. No; they refused. I climbed up in their limbs, imploring. They were silent. I was angered and made a fool of myself beating on the trunks with my fists screaming, "Tell me about the bird! It is only a bird!"

Learning your dreams unnerved me. What unholy trespass I had made.

When I regained my composure I apologized, touching the maple trunks gently with my fingers. As I departed a wind moved the leaves of a low branch against my face and I was embarrassed, for I was waiting for some sign of understanding. I walked on, alert now to the wind showing here and there in the grass. The wind suddenly spoke of you as of a father. The thoughts were incomplete, hinting at something incomprehensible, ungraspable, but I learned this: you are able to stand in the river in such a way that the wind makes no sound against you. You arrange yourself so that you cast no shadow and you stop breathing for half an hour. The only sound is the faint movement of your blood. You are quiet enough to hear fish swimming toward you.

When I asked, discretely, whether long ago you might

have fought someone, some enemy whose name I might recognize, the wind was suddenly no longer there. From such strength as is in you I suspect an enemy. I have inquired of the stones at the bottom of the river; I have inquired of your other enemy, the pine marten; I have waded silently with your relatives, the bitterns, alert for any remarks, all to no avail.

I have been crippled by my age, by what I have known, as well as by my youth, by what I have yet to learn, in all these inquiries. It has taken me years, which might have been spent (by someone else) seeking something greater, in some other place. I have sought only you. Enough. I wish to know you, and you will not speak.

It is not easy to tell the rest, but I know you have heard it from others. Now I wish you to hear it from me. I took bits of bone from fish you had eaten and pierced my fingers, letting the blood trail away in the current. I slept on what feathers of yours I could find. From a tree felled in a storm I took your nest, climbed with it to a clearing above the river where there was a good view, as much sky as I could comprehend. Bear grass, pentstemon, blue gilia, wild strawberries, Indian paintbrush growing there. Each night for four nights I made a small fire with sticks from the old nest and looked out toward the edge of the shadows it threw. On the last night I had a great dream. You were standing on a desert plain. You were painted blue and you wore a necklace of white salmon vertebrae. Your eyes huge, red. Before you on the dry, gray earth a snake coiled, slowly weaving the air with his head. You spoke about the beginning of the world, that there was going to be no fear in the world, that everything that was afraid would live poorly.

8

The snake said coldly, weaving, yes, there would be fear, that fear would make everything strong, and lashed out, opening a wound in your shoulder. As fast, you pinned his head to the ground and said—the calmness in your voice—fear might come, and it could make people strong, but it would be worth nothing without compassion. And you released the snake.

I awoke sprawled in bear grass. It was darker than I could ever remember a night being. I felt the spot on the planet where I lay, turned away from the sun. My legs ached. I knew how old I was lying there on the top of the mountain, a fist of cold air against my breast as some animal, a mouse perhaps, moved suddenly under my back.

An unpronounceable forgiveness swept over me. I knew how much had to be given away, how little could ever be asked. The sound of geese overhead in the darkness just then, and all that it meant, was enough.

I leap into the jade color of the winter river. I fight the current to reach the rocks, climb up on them and listen for the sound of your voice. I stand dripping, shivering in my white nakedness, in the thin dawn light. Waiting. Silent. You begin to appear at a downriver bend.

THE
LOG JAM

1946

In September, when bearberry leaves were ready to pick, after the first storm had come upvalley like a drunken miner headed home, snapping limbs as thick as your arms off the maples, Olin Sanders caught a big tree barberchairing and was dead before they could get him out of the woods. They laid him across the laps of two men in the back of the truck and sent word ahead. When they got down to the road his wife was there crying, with pink curlers like pine cones in her hair and in black knit slacks too small for her stout legs and a loose hanging white blouse. And two county sheriffs, drawn by the word of death, wearing clean, pressed clothing, like clerks. When she looked in through the window of the truck and saw him broken in half like a buckled tin can she raised her fists to beat at the thing responsible and began beating the truck. When the sheriff held her back and said in a polite voice, "Now, control yourself," she began beating her thighs. One of the men stepped up and punched the sheriff.

All this time the son, in whose lap the father's broken head was cradled, sat silent. He was aware of the beginning of something else, more than his father's end. His pants were wet with his father's blood.

That night the boy left the house, walked past his father's

shirts hanging to dry on the line, and drove up the Warner Creek Road to the place where they had been cutting. He sidestepped downslope with the chainsaw in his hands to reach the stump of the tree (the blood congealed like dark sap on the wood) and cut it off, cut off the top of the stump with the stain of his father's death on it, the saw screaming in the dim night. With a choker and a length of cable he hauled the butt round uphill and cursed and jacked it into the back of his pickup.

He came off Warner Mountain to the Granite Creek Road and went down Granite Creek until he came to the equipment shed, where a logging bridge crossed the river to the highway side. With a front loader and a length of chain he yanked the slab of wood out of the pickup, drove out onto the bridge and with jerking motions and the hiss of hydraulics he twisted the machine crosswise, tipped the bucket and dumped the slab of fir into the river.

He put the front loader away and drove home.

No one had ever done anything like this before. The lack of any tradition in it bothered the boy. As he walked past the trees near the house he was suddenly afraid. His mother was awake, sitting in the darkened living room when he walked in, wearing the tattered quilt robe that embarrassed him when his friends were around. Behind the glow of her cigarette she asked where he had been.

The butt round came back to the surface of the river, the thunderous sound of its plunge evaporating in the night, and it moved off like a dark iceberg riding low in the water. A few miles and it beached quietly on the cobbles of an island.

1951

Cawley Besson and his family—a wife called June, two boys, and a mixed-breed dog—came to work for the Forest Service. There was timber then, timber uncruised in backcountry valleys. Douglas firs ten feet through at the base and straight-grained for two hundred and fifty feet. Dense, slow-grown wood. It was show-off timber and no need to spare it.

Cawley opened roads to it. He was tight-bellied, dedicated, and clipped in his manners. He left early for work and came home late, with a reputation, he said, to think about. He had places to go after this job he told his wife (lying next to him, listening to him, wondering when they would make love again), places to go.

On a hot Sunday in June, Cawley sat at the river's edge in a pair of shorts, eating a picnic lunch, thinking about Monday, drinking cold beer and watching his sons. The boys were throwing rocks into the river, which the dog chased until he felt the current at his legs and stepped back. Cawley liked the feel of this: he looked toward his wife, feeling the warmth of his own body. The boy swept past him, gesticulating silently, before the scream arrived in his ears, as the dog ran over him barking, and he looked to see the other son standing motionless at the river's edge with his hands over his mouth.

Cawley leaped to his feet, spilling food away, calling out, running to catch up, cursing jibberish. He could not swim, the boy either. He saw the small white face in the dark water, the sunlight bright in his short wet hair, and what lay ahead began to close in on him. The boy, wide-eyed and quiet, went with the river.

Cawley continued to run. The panic got into him like leeches. The beer was coming up acid in his mouth. The river bore the boy on and he calculated how fast, running harder to get ahead, yelling to the boy Hold on! Hold on! Jesus hold on. A little ahead now. He saw the vine maple coming at him, grabbed it, bent it, broke it so fast he felt hope, ran hard into the shallows ahead of the boy to throw the end of the long branch to him—who spun off its tip with his hands splayed, rigid. Cawley dropped the limb and churning high-legged and mad, chest deep and with a sudden plunge had the boy, had his shirt, and was flailing for shore, grabbing for rocks in the river bed that swept by under him. His feet touched ground and held. His fist was white with his grip twisted in the boy's tee-shirt—the boy could hardly breathe against his clutch.

The maple limb drifted downriver and came to rest among willows, near a log round on which dark stains were still visible.

1954

A storm came this year, against which all other storms were to be measured, on a Saturday in October, a balmy afternoon. Men in the woods cutting firewood for winter, and children outside with melancholy thoughts lodged somewhere in the memory of summer. It built as it came up the valley as did every fall storm, but the steel-gray thunderheads, the first sign of it anyone saw, were higher, much higher, too high. In the stillness before it hit, men looked at each other as though a fast and wiry man had pulled a knife in a bar. They felt the trees falling before they heard the wind, and they dropped tools and scrambled to get out. The wind came up suddenly and like a

16

scythe, like piranha after them, like seawater through a breach in a dike. The first blow bent trees half to the ground, the second caught them and snapped them like kindling, sending limbs raining down and twenty-foot splinters hurtling through the air like mortar shells to stick quivering in the ground. Bawling cattle running the fences, a loose lawnmower bumping across a lawn, a stray dog lunging for a child racing by. The big trees went down screaming, ripping open holes in the wind that were filled with the broken-china explosion of a house and the yawing screech of a pickup rubbed across asphalt, the rivet popping and twang of phone and electric wires.

It was over in three or four minutes. The eerie, sucking silence it left behind seemed palpably evil, something that would get into the standing timber, like insects, a memory.

No one was killed. Roads were cut off, a bridge buckled. No power. A few had to walk in from places far off in the steep wooded country, arriving home later than they'd ever been up. Some said it pulled the community together, others how they hated living in the trees with no light. No warning. The next day it rained and the woods smelled like ashes. It was four or five days before they got the roads opened and the phones working, electricity back. Three sent down to the hospital in Holterville. Among the dead, Cawley Besson's dog. And two deer, butchered and passed quietly in parts among neighbors.

Of the trees that fell into the river, a number came up like beached whales among willows at the tip of an island.

1957

Rebecca Grayson drove forty-one miles each morning to

work in a men's clothing store in town and came back each evening in time to fix her husband's dinner. It was a job that had paid for births and funerals, for weddings and a second automobile but it left her depressed and stranded now, at fifty-six, as if it were a clear defeat, invisible but keenly known to her.

Her husband operated a gas station and logging supply shop in Beaver Creek, a small town on the river. They had had four daughters, which had caused Clarence Grayson a kind of dismay from which he never recovered. It wasn't a country for raising daughters, he thought. He lived as though he were waiting for wounds to heal before moving on.

He hardly noticed, when she helped him in the shop on Saturdays, that someone often came by with wildflowers for her, or to tell a story, to ask had she seen the skunk cabbage in Danmeier's field or the pussy willows blooming, sure signs of spring. Clarence appreciated these acts of kindness, while he finished a job for whoever it was, as a duty done that he had no way with.

Men were attracted to Rebecca in an innocent but almost hungry way, as though needing the pleasure she took in them. Because there was never a hint of anything but friendship, their attentions both pleased her and left her with a deep longing, out of which, unashamed, she lay awake at night in a self-embrace of fantasy.

Late at night, when he couldn't sleep, Clarence would roll over to her and try to speak. Sometimes he would begin to cry and sob in anger at a loss he couldn't find the words for. He cried against her negligee and drove his fist weakly into his pillow. On those nights she held him until the pain ran its course, and said nothing of her own yearning.

After the last daughter had married she thought they could go away. In a deeply private place she wished to go to Europe, alone; but she could not bear the thought of his loneliness and did not believe that in a journey together there could be any joy.

One summer evening while Clarence was in the living room reading, she sat on their bed with her face lowered to a glass bowl of dried blossoms in her lap, a pool of musky odor that triggered memory and passion in her and to which she would touch her face in moments when she needed friendship. Twenty years of anniversary roses, flowers from her first gardens, wildflowers from men who were charmed by her, a daughter's wedding bouquet. She felt the tears run the length of her nose and the tightness of her small fists pressing against her knees. She wished to be rid of it, and she rose with the bowl and left.

In the dark yard by the side of the house she took off her dress and her soft underclothes. With the bowl firmly in her grip she walked down to the river and stepped in. The cold water rose against her as she moved away from the shore, lapped at her pale belly, and she felt a resolve as strong as any love she could ever remember. Her breasts hardened in the cold air. Waist deep in the water, her feet bent painfully around the stones (on the far bank she could see into the living rooms of people she knew), she scattered the first handful on the water. The pieces landed soundlessly and teetered quickly away. She flung the dry petals, the shrunken blossoms and the discolored flakes until the bowl was empty, and then dipped its lip to the current to swirl it clean.

She stood there, numb to the cold, until the wind had dissipated the perfume, listening to the wash around her hips, feeling the excitement of something she could not grasp. She thought of herself going on, like the river, without a break, with two herons flying overhead, untouchable and graceful, toward an undetermined destination. She had no wish to explain the feeling to anyone.

Of the flowers she threw on the water, some floated down as far as the log jam and hung up in its crevices.

1964

By this time beaver had come back to the valley, once having been trapped out. They were few and save for the sight of alders cut along the creeks their lives went unnoticed. One of the dams blocked a feeder stream above Bear Creek and was found one morning in the fall by a boy hunting deer. He walked across, testing it idly as he went, then throwing his weight to it, trying to make it spring. He came to a halt and surveyed the dam with surprise, for it did not give. On the far side he set his gun against a tree and cut an alder pole, stripping the leaves and sharpening the point with swift, deft strokes of his knife. Walking back across the span he began to probe the structure, looking for an opening with depth. He found such a place and twisting the pole into it began to pry and root with the tip, seeking better leverage. Bracing his legs and putting all the strength of his back and upper arms into it, he broke out a wedge of mud and twigs. Against this breach he began to use the pole like a post-hole digger, raising it above his head and ramming deeper and deeper, prying against any purchase. The green twigs were supple and difficult to break so he turned to the knife. Cut through, then pry. He was beginning to sweat.

As he took off his jacket he saw the beaver surface in the middle of the pond. He hunkered quietly off the dam and hid in the brush. The beaver, motionless in the center of departing concentric rings of water, followed each movement.

The boy stared at the beaver, angry for having allowed himself to be seen. He could feel his heart pounding, the sudden compression of his muscles, smell his own warm odors. His hand located a rock. In one fluid motion he rose to fire it with tremendous strength, so hard the hair jumped on his head with the snap of his body. He missed. The beaver slipped under. He picked up another rock. *Twoosh*. The sound of the stone cutting into the pond steadied him. *Twoosh. Twoosh.*

He returned to the dam, to the place where he had gouged an opening. Prying, batting, cutting, and kicking; finally, against a fulcrum of boulders carried from the shore, he broke through the mesh of limbs. He stepped aside, disheveled. As the water flowed cleanly through the cut he came to realize the break was too shallow, only several inches below the surface of the pond; and that it was too late in the day to go hunting. And that the beaver had not shown himself again. He cursed the beaver, threw the pry pole into the pond and, taking his gun, walked off sullenly.

The pond drained to the level of the cut. After dark the beaver came to the breach and began to weave a closure.

The boy threatened to return to the valley and trap beaver that winter but did not.

Alder branches from the dam were swept down Bear Creek and into the river, where they wedged in the log jam.

1973

The fir that grew next to the Thompson's house was, by a count of its rings, 447 years old when it fell at dusk on a March day during dinner. Before it fell the sounds outside were only those of the river coming up softly through the trees and the calls of grosbeaks. Gene Thompson was able to hear other things as he sat at the table. He could hear trees growing and dying. (When he walked in the woods he could distinguish between the creaking of cedar and the creaking of hemlock, between the teeter of rocks in a stream and the heartbeat of a spotted owl. He lay in the woods with his ear pressed to the damp earth listening to the slow burrowing of tree roots, which he distinguished from the digging of moles or worms, or the sound of rivers moving deep in the earth.) When he listened with his forehead against a tree he heard the thinking of woodpeckers asleep inside. He heard the flow of sap which sounded like stratospheric winds to him.

Gene sat quietly at dinner listening to the fir by the house. He heard the sudden spread of a filigree of cracks in the termite-ridden roots, the groaning of fibers stretched as the tree shifted its weight, seventy tons, toward the river and a muffled popping in the earth as it gave way. He heard (the fork poised before his mouth) the sweeping brush of trailing limbs high overhead as it began its descent. With the first loud crack, the terrible whining screech of separation, the gasping, sucking noise in its wake as the tree sailed down, everyone looked up. The tree struck the earth like a sheet of iron and dinner leaped from the table. A soft after-rain of twigs.

Gene went out the door with his father.

"Holy cow!" he said, striding toward it.

It had taken other trees with it, broken the highway and lay with its top in the river. It had to be removed, said his father, right away, to let traffic through. "Six or seven feet," he said to an approaching neighbor, "through the butt and clean for two hundred feet." Lucky no one had been killed, he said. He knew its value. Prime old growth. Overmature. Cut right it could be worth $3,000. He figured it roughly, climbed up on it and paced off a measurement in the falling light while another son jerked a chain saw to life to begin to clear the road.

The boy squatted at the stump with his hands spread wide in the tawny sap. He had heard the slow movement of air through the lengthening termite tunnels and had known. He raised his hands from the stump and the sap hung stiffly from his fingers like spirals of honey.

The crown of the tree eventually washed downriver and became entangled at the tip of the island. In the years that followed a pair of osprey came and built a nest, and lived as well as could be expected in that country.

THE
BEND

In the evenings I walk down and stand in the trees, in light paused just so in the leaves, as if the change in the river here were not simply known to me but apprehended. It did not start out this way; I began with the worst sort of ignorance, the grossest inquiries. Now I ask very little. I observe the swift movement of water through the nation of fish at my feet. I wonder privately if there are for them, as there are for me, moments of faith.

The river comes around from the southeast to the east at this point: a clean shift of direction, water deep and fast on the outside of the curve, flowing slower over the lip of a broad gravel bar on the inside, continuing into a field of shattered boulders to the west.

I kneel and slip my hands like frogs beneath the surface of the water. I feel the wearing away of the outer edge, the exposure of rootlets, the undermining. I imagine eyes in the tips of my fingers, like the eyestalks of crayfish. Fish stare at my fingertips and bolt into the river's darkness. I withdraw my hands, conscious of the trespass. The thought that I might be observed disturbs me.

I've wanted to take the measure of this turn in the river, grasp it for private reasons. I feel closer to it now. I know which deer drink at which spots on this bank. I know of the small screech owl nesting opposite (I would point him out to you by throwing a stone in that direction but the gesture would not be appropriate). I am familiar with the raccoon and fisher whose tracks appear here, can even tell them apart in the dark by delicately fingering the rim of their prints in the soil. I can hear the preparations of muskrats. On cold, damp nights I am aware of the fog of birds' breath that rolls oceanic through the trees above. Out there, I know which rocks are gripped by slumbering water striders, and where beneath the water lie the slipcase homes of caddis fly larvae.

I feel I am coming closer to it.

For myself, each day more of me slips away. Absorbed in seeing how the water comes through the bend, just so, I am myself, sliding off.

The attempt to wrestle meaning from this spot began poorly, with illness. A pain, slow in coming like so many, that seemed centered in the back of my neck. Then an acute yearning, as strong as the wish to be loved, pain along the ribs, and my legs started to give way. I awoke in the morning with my hands over my face as though astonished by my own dreams. As the weeks went on I moved about less and less, until finally I went to bed and lay there like summer leaves. I could hear the rain in the woods in the afternoon; the sound of the river, like the laughing of horses; smell faintly through the open window the breath of bears. Between these points I was contained, closed off like a spider by the design of a web. I tried to imagine that I was well, but the points of my imagination impaled me, and then a sense of betrayal emptied me.

I began to think (as on a staircase descending to an unexamined basement) about the turn in the river. If I could understand this smoothly done change of direction I could imitate it, I reasoned, just as a man puts what he reads in a story to use, substituting one point for another as he needs.

Several things might be measured I speculated: the rate of flow of the water, the erosion of the outer bank, the slope of the adjacent mountains, the changing radius of curvature as the river turned west. It could be revealed neatly, affirmed with graphic authority.

I became obsessed with its calculation. I lay the plan out first in my head, without recourse to paper. The curve required calculus, and so some loss of accuracy; and the precise depth of the river changed from moment to moment, as did its width. But I could abide this for the promise of insight into my life.

I called on surveyors, geodesic scientists, hydrologists. It was the work of half a year. It involved them in the arduous toting of instruments back and forth across the river and in tedious calculation. I asked that exacting journals be kept, that no scrap of description be lost. There were arguments, of course. I required that renderings be done again, over and over. I became convinced that in this wealth of detail a fixed reason for the river's graceful turn would inevitably be revealed.

The workmen, defeated by the precision required, in an anger all their own, hurled their theodolites into the trees. (The repair of these instruments consumed more time.) I understood that fights broke out. But I saw none of this. I lay alone in the room and those in my employ came and went politely with their notes. I knew they thought it pointless, but there was their own employment to be considered, and they said the wage was fair.

Finally they reduced the bend in the river to an elegant

series of equations, and the books containing them and a bewildering list of variables were all gathered together and brought to my room. I had them placed on the floor, stacked in a corner. I suddenly had the strength for the first time, staring at this pile, to move, but I was afraid. I put it off until morning; I felt my recovery was certain, believed even more forcefully now that my own resolution was at hand by an incontestable analogy.

That night I awoke to hear the dripping of water. From the direction of the pile of notes came the sound of mergansers, the explosive sound they make when they are surprised on the water and suddenly fly off.

I lay back.

Moss grew eventually on the books. They began after a while to harden, to resemble the gray boulders in the river. Years passed. I smelled cottonwood on spring afternoons, and would imagine sunshine crinkling on the surface of the water.

In winter the windows remained open because I could not reach them.

One morning, without warning, I came to a dead space in my depression, a sudden horizontal view, which I seized. I pried myself from the room, coming down the stairs slow step by slow step, all the while calling out. Bears heard me (or were already waiting at the door). I told them I needed to be near the river. They carried me through the trees (growling, for they are not used to working together), throwing their shoulders to the alders until we stood at the outer bank.

Then they departed, leaving the odor of bruised grass and cracked bone hanging in the air.

The first thing I did was to feel, raccoonlike, with the tips of my fingers the soil of the bank just below the water's edge. I listened for the sound of water on the outer bar. I observed the hunt of the caddis fly.

I am now taking the measure of the bend in these experiences.

I have lost, as I have said, some sense of myself. I no longer require as much. And though I am hopeful of recovery, an adjustment as smooth as the way the river lies against the earth at this point, this is no longer the issue with me. I am more interested in this: from above, to a hawk, the bend must appear only natural and I for the moment inseparably a part, like salmon or a flower. I cannot say well enough how this single perception has dismantled my loneliness.

THE
FALLS

Someone must see to it that this story is told: you shouldn't think this man just threw his life away.

When he was a boy there was nothing about him to remember. He looked like anything else—like the trees, like other people, like his dog. The dog was part coyote. Sometimes he would change places with his dog. For a week at a time he was the dog and the dog was himself, and it went by unnoticed. It was harder on the dog, but the boy encouraged him and he did well at it. The dog's name was Leaves.

When the boy went to sleep in the hills he would become the wind or a bird flying overhead. It was, again, harder on the dog, running to keep up, but the dog knew the boy would be a man someday and would no longer want to be a bird or the wind, or even a half-breed dog like himself, but himself. Above all, the dog trusted in time.

This is what happened. The boy grew. Visions came to him. He began to see things. When he was eighteen he dreamed he should go up in the Crazy Mountains north of Big Timber to dream, and he went. He was careful from whom he took rides. Old cars. Old men only. He was old enough to be careful but not to know why.

The dreaming was four days. I do not know what came to him. He told no one. He spoke with no one. While he was up there the dog, Leaves, slept out on some rocks in the Sweetgrass

River, where he would not be bothered, and fasted. I came at dawn and then at dusk to look. I could not tell from a distance if he was asleep or dead. Or about the dog. I would only know it was all right because each morning he was in a different position. The fourth morning—I remember this one the best, the sun like fire on the October trees, so many spider webs sunken under the load of dew, the wind in them, as though the trees were breathing—he was gone. I swam out to see about the dog. Wild iris petals there on the green moss. That was a good dog.

The man was back home in two days. He washed in the river near his home.

He got a job down there around Beatty and I didn't see him for two or three years. The next time was in winter. It was the coldest one I had ever been in. Chickadees froze. The river froze all the way across. I never saw that before. I picked him up hitchhiking north. He had on dark cotton pants and a light jacket and lace shoes. With a brown canvas bag and a hat pulled down over his ears and his hands in his pockets. I pulled over right away. He looked sorry as hell.

I took him all the way up north, to my place. He had some antelope meat with him and we ate good. That was the best meat I ever had. We talked. He wanted to know what I was doing for work. I was cutting wood. He was going to go up to British Columbia, Nanaimo, in there, in spring to look for work. That night when we were going to bed I saw his back in the kerosene light. The muscles looked like water coming over his shoulders and going into the bed of his spine. I went over and hugged him.

I woke up the next morning when it was just getting light. I could not hear the sound of the river and the silence frightened me until I remembered. I heard chopping on the ice. I got dressed and went down. The earth was like rock that winter.

He had cut a hole a few feet across, black water boiling up, flowing out on the ice, freezing. He was standing in the hole naked with his head bowed and his arms straight up over his head with his hands open. He had cut his arms with a knife and the red blood was running down them, down his ribs, slowing in the cold, to the black water. I could see his body shaking, the muscles starting to go blue-gray over his bones, the color of the ice. He called out in a voice so strong I sat down as though his voice had hit me. I had never heard a cry like that, his arms down and his fists squeezed tight, his mouth, those large white teeth, his forehead knotted. The cry was like a bear, not a man sound, like something he was tearing away from inside himself.

The cry went up like a roar and fell away into a trickle, like creek water over rocks at the end of summer. He was bent over with his lips near the water. His fist opened. He put water to his lips four times, and washed the blood off. He leaped out of that hole like a salmon and ran off west, around the bend, gone into the trees, very high steps.

I went down to look at the blood on the gray-white ice.

He cut wood with me that winter. He worked hard. When the trillium bloomed and the varied thrushes came he went north.

I did not see him again for ten years. I was in North Dakota harvesting wheat, sleeping in the back of my truck (parked under cottonwoods for the cool air that ran down their trunks at night like water). One night I heard my name. He was by the tailgate.

"You got a good spot," he said.

"Yeah. That you?"

"Sure."

"How you doing?"

"Good. Talk in the morning."

He sounded tired, like he'd been riding all day.

Next morning someone left, too much drinking, and he got that job, and so we worked three weeks together, clear up into Saskatchewan, before we turned around and drove home. When we came through Stanley Basin in Idaho we crossed over a little bridge where the Salmon River was only a foot deep, ten feet across. It came across a big meadow, out of some quaking aspen. "Let's go up there," he said. "I bet that's good water." We did. We camped up in those aspen and that was good water. It was sweet like a woman's lips when you are in love and holding back.

We came home and he stayed with me that winter, too. I was getting old then and it was good he was around. In the spring he left. He told me a lot that winter, but I can't say these things. When he spoke about them it was like the breeze when you are asleep in the woods: you listen hard, but it is not easy. It is not your language. He lived in the desert near antelope one year, by a lake where geese came in the spring. The antelope taught him to run. The geese did not teach him anything, he said, but it was good to be around them. The water in the lake was so clear when the geese floated they seemed to be suspended, twenty or twenty-five feet off the ground.

The morning he left the desert he took a knife and carefully scraped his whole body. He put some of these small pieces of skin in the water and scattered the rest over the sagebrush.

He went to work then in another town in Nevada some-where, I forget, in a lumberyard and he was there for a long time, five or six years. He took time off a lot, went into the mountains for a few weeks, a place where he could see the sun come up and go down. Clean out everything bad that had built up.

When he left that place he went to Alaska, around Anchorage somewhere, but couldn't find any work and ended up at Sitka fishing and then went to Matanuska Valley, working on a farm there. All that time he was alone. Once he came down to see me but I was gone. I knew it when I got home. I went down to the river and saw the place where he went into the water. The ground was soft around the rocks. I knew his feet. I am not a man of great power, but I took what I had and gave it to him that time, everything I had. "You keep going," I said. I raised my hands over my head and stepped into the water and shouted it again, "You keep going!" My heart was pounding like a waterfall.

That time after he left he was gone almost ten years again. I had a dream he was living up on those salmon rivers in the north. I don't know. Maybe it was a no-account dream. I knew he never went south.

Last time I saw him he came to my house in the fall. He came in quiet as air sitting in a canyon. We made dinner early and at dusk he went out and I followed him because I knew he wanted me to. He cut twigs from the ash and cottonwood and alder and I got undressed. He brushed my body with these bank-growing trees and said I had always been a good friend. He said this was his last time. We went swimming a little. There is a good current at that place. It is hard to swim.

39

Later we went up to the house and ate. He told me a story about an old woman who tried to keep two husbands and stories about a man who couldn't sing but went around making people pay to hear him sing anyway. I laughed until I was tired out and went to bed.

I woke up suddenly, at the end of a dream. It was the same dream I had once before, about him climbing up a waterfall out of the sky. I went to look in his bed. He was gone. I got dressed and drove my truck to the falls below the willow flats where I killed my first deer many years ago. I ran into the trees, fighting the vine maple and deadfalls, running now as hard as I could for the river. The thunder of that falls was all around me and the ground shaking. I came out on the river, slipping on the black rocks glistening in the moonlight. I saw him all at once standing at the lip of the falls. I began to shiver in the damp cold, the mist stinging my face, moonlight on the water when I heard that bear-sounding cry and he was shaking up there at the top of the falls, silver like a salmon shaking, and that cry louder than the falls for a moment, and then swallowed and he was in the air, turning over and over, moonlight finding the silver-white of his sides and dark green back before he cut into the water, the sound lost in the roar.

I did not want to leave. Sunrise. I went up onto the willow flats where I could see the sky. I felt the sunlight going deep into my hair. Good fall day. Good day to go look for chinquapin nuts, but I sat down and fell asleep.

When I awoke it was late. I went back to my truck and drove home. On the way I was wondering if I felt strong enough to eat salmon.

THE
SHALLOWS

The overall impression here, as one surveys the river spread out over the gravel bars, is of a suspension of light, as though light were reverberating on a membrane. And a loss of depth. The slope of the riverbed here is nearly level, so the movement of water slows; shallowness heightens the impression of transparency and a feeling for the texture of the highly polished stones just underwater. If you bring your eye to within a few inches of the surface, each stone appears to be submerged in glycerin yet still sharply etched, as if held closely under a strong magnifying glass in summer light. An illusion—that insight into the stone is possible, that all distraction can be peeled away or masked off, as in preparation for surgery, while sunlight penetrates and highlights—is encouraged.

Beyond the light, a loss of depth, as the subsurface nears the surface, as though the river were exposing itself to examination. Kneel with your ear to the water; beyond the *plorp* of it in a hollow and the slooshing gurgle through labyrinthine gravels, are the more distant sound of its fugue. A musical notebook lies open—alto and soprano clefs, notes tied and trills, turned notes, indications of arpeggio and glissando. Plunge your ear in suddenly—how it vanishes. Take the surface of the river between your thumb and forefinger. These textures are exquisite, unexpected.

Step back. The light falling on the dry rocks beneath our feet seems leathery by comparison. And this is another difference: the light on the dry rock is direct, shaftlike, almost brutal, so rigid one can imagine a sound like crystal lightly stung with a fingernail if it were touched; while the cooler light on the rocks in the water is indirect, caressing. This is why if you pluck a stone from the water and allow it to dry it seems to shrivel. It is the same as that phenomenon where at dusk you are able to see more clearly at the periphery of your vision. An indirect approach, the sidelong glance of the sun through the water, coaxes out the full character of the naturally reticent stone.

Fish are most exposed in the shallows, and so move through quickly. One afternoon I saw an osprey here, reminiscent of a grizzly at the water's edge anticipating salmon. A fish came by; he took off lightly and snatched it from the water.

Here, step across; you'll be able to examine things better out on the gravel bars. (We are fortunate for the day—temperatures in the eighties I understand.) Look, now at the variety of stones. Viewed from the bank these gravel bars seem uniformly gray, but bend close and you see this is not true. It's as though at first glance nothing were given away. You could regard this as the stone's effort to guard against intrusion by the insincere. Here, look at these: the red, chert, a kind of quartz; this streaked gray, basalt; the greenish one, a sedimentary rock, shale, stained with copper; the blue—this is uncommon: chrysocolla, a silicate. The white, quartzite. Obsidian. Black glass. This brown, andesite. It's reassuring to hear the names, but it's not so important to remember them. It's more important to see that these are pieces of the earth, reduced, ground down to an essential statement, that in our lifetime they are irreducible. This is one of the differences between, say, stones and flowers.

I used to throw a few stones out into the river—underhand with a flick of the wrist, like this.

It is relatively simple, in a place where the river slows like this, fans out over the gravel, to examine aspects of its life, to come to some understanding of its history. See, for example, where this detritus has caught in the rocks? Raccoon whisker. Hemlock twig. Dead bumblebee. Deer-head orchid. Maidenhair fern. These are dry willow leaves of some sort. There are so many willows, all of which can interbreed. Trying to hold each one to a name is like trying to give a name to each rill trickling over the bar here, and making it stick. Who is going to draw the lines? And yet it is done. Somewhere this leaf has a name, *Salix hookeriana*, *Salix lasiandra*.

Piece of robin's egg, perhaps after a raid by a long-tailed weasel. Chip of yew tree bark. Fireweed. Snail shell—made out of the same thing as your fingernail. Here, tap it—Or a rattle-snake's rattles. Roll it around in your hand. Imagine the clues in just this. Counting the rings would tell you something, but no one is sure what. Perhaps all that is recorded is the anguish of snails. Oh, this is rare: fox hairs. You can tell by the coloring. Some say it is the degree of taper, the shape. Up above some-place a fox crossed over. Or was killed by someone.

Behind the larger stones—let's walk up this way—hung up in their crevices is another kind of detritus entirely, a layer of understanding that becomes visible only under certain cir-cumstances, often after a thunderstorm, for example, when the air has a sudden three-dimensional quality and it appears it might be slit open neatly and examined from the inside. What you see then, tethered to the rocks as though floating on the silken threads of spider webs adrift in the balmy air, are the sighs of sparrows passing overhead. The jubilation of wind-touched aspens. The persistence of crayfish, the tentative sipping of deer, who have stepped clear of the cover of trees, the circumspection of lone fish.

And there are still other revelations beyond these. You can imagine what might be learned in a place like this if one took the time. Think only of the odors, some single strand of which might be nipped between rocks, of wildflowers (lupine, avalanche lily, the white blossoms of bunchberry, yellow balsamroot, crimson currant), of musk (needle-toothed weasel, sleek-furred mink, bright-eyed fisher, grizzly bear on his rump, eating the seed pods of dogtooth violet), of suncracked earth, the odor of granite. Just so, by these invisible extensions is the character of the river revealed, is there some clue to what goes unexamined.

If you lie out flat on the stones—it seems odd to try, I know—you will feel—here, that's it—the warmth of the sunlight emanating from the stones. Turn your head to the side, ear to rock, and you will hear the earth revolving on its axis and an adjustment of stones in the riverbed. The heartbeats of salmon roe. One day I heard the footsteps of someone miles away, following someone else.

If you look up into the sky, straight up, eight or ten miles, it is possible to imagine the atmospheric tides, oceans of air moving against the edge of space in an ebb and flow as dependent on the phases of the moon. I believe lying here on the gravel bars cannot be too different from lying on your back on the bottom of the ocean. You can choose to take this view or not, with no fear of consequence. The tides go on, regardless.

Let's walk along the edge.

The fish this garter snake has just snatched is called a dace, a relative of the creek chub, a life more obscure than most. The snake is *Thamnophis couchi hydrophila*, a western species. You can take the naming as far as you want. Some of the most enjoyable things—the way the water folds itself around that rock and drops away—have no names.

You are beginning to shiver, but it's nothing to be alarmed over. The stones warmed you; you sensed you were nestled in the earth. When you stood up fear pooled in an exposed feeling around your back. This is what to leave the earth means. To stand up, which you see bears do on occasion. At the very heart of this act is the meaning of personal terror.

Along the very edge of these gravel bars are some of the earth's seams. A person with great courage and balance could slip between the water and the rock, the wet and the dry, and perhaps never come back. But I think it must take as much courage to stay.

I have stood for hours on these gravel bars. I have seen the constellations reflected in chips of obsidian glass. My hands have gone out to solitary willows in the darkness. Once I lay without moving for days until, mistaking me for driftwood, birds landed nearby and began speaking in murmurs of Pythagoras and winds that blew in the Himalayas.

I regretted throwing stones into the river.

THE
RAPIDS

Please. Stand back.

Could you tell me if there was any trace of the boat?

No. That is—please. No one knows.

Are the men all presumed dead?

The children. Jesus, these people must have had children.

I wonder if I could get a word with you.

The river is like hell here.

You mean—

Should cover them with a tarp.

I've lived here all my life.

Yes?

And each year it happens like this. If not here, then some-where else.

I'll bet there were three of them in the boat when it hit the logs.

Yeah. I'd expect.

Seventeen people here since 1970.

Should shut it down. State should.

Excuse me, would you say the river, well, a violent river like this, exacts a toll?

What?

Do people pay a price to use this river?

Mister, if a tree fell on you, would you say the forest was taking a toll?

What I meant—

Someday you might drown. You want your wife to say he paid the price?

And when you least expect it too, bub, just like these fellows.

These guys sure as hell knew it was dangerous to go into these rapids.

Went in, nevertheless.

Paid for it too.

That's what I meant.

We ain't talking the same price.

Excuse me, sir, did you see the accident?

No.

Well could you tell me what you know about it?

You ought to write down Collier Rapids. That's what the name of the place is.

Would you—I wonder if there are any members of the family you could point out here.

Jesus, look at the water come through that chute.

How old is this man? Twenty-four? Twenty-five? What a waste. And look at the wedding ring. He's married.

You know I hate to see anyone die. There's no need.

If you try on this side it ain't so bad, but you try on the other side and you whittled your last stick.

Mister, there wasn't anybody here when it happened. If you want to figure it all out why don't you just walk over there and look. You could throw a locomotive in that hole and never find it again.

Excuse me, do you live around here?

No, I was driving by.

Could you step back please, sir?

This guy's trying to write a story by talking to people who ain't got no answers. You ought to get yourself a boat and get out there. That's all the answer you'll need.

There's no need to yell at me. People have drowned here. Someone said seventeen in the last few years. This is a terrible thing. It makes people very sad.

River's the one sad.

My Lord, look how white his hands are. Why don't they put a jacket over his face.

Officer, I believe one of these poor men was at Nesmith's station last night. In a pickup pulling a boat. Had a kind of collie dog with him.

You're looking for someone to explain a couple of dead men and what's left of a boat.

The boat? Where?

There, in the water.

People want to be informed.

About these dead people and a broken boat? What are they gonna learn?

You ought to tell them to stay away from what they don't understand. These guys went in to the wrong chute. Won't work when the water's this high.

You got to know what you're doing.

Look, tore his shoes off. And I just—oh my—I just bought my husband a pair of pants like that. I'm taking them right back.

Can you imagine what they thought when they knew they were wrong, how lonely it must have been?

Pardon me, did you know these people?

Me?

Yes.

No.

Well several people have drowned here in the last few years. I wonder if you've ever been involved in a rescue—I presume this is your home here.

Yes. My wife drowned here in 1947.

You were present?

We were fishing on those rocks up above. Current pulled our boat away and we were stuck. We couldn't swim, either of us. We tried to get back, jumping from rock to rock. We'd slip and get swept farther downriver each time. I'd grab a rock, she'd grab my foot. She was a small woman, no bigger than this. Pulled me by the hair, right out of the mouth of one of those chutes. We were trapped on a small rock and it got dark. We knew no one was going to come that far down in a boat. We lay there shivering all night. In the morning it seemed the water had dropped some. We decided to wait until the afternoon. We sat there holding hands. I wanted to try it alone, come back with help somehow. It came time and we hugged. I jumped in and I heard her jump in suddenly upstream of me. She had hold of me for a moment and then was gone. I reached shore. I never saw her again. I ran below, along the bank, calling her name. I looked for her for days.

I'm sorry to hear that.

Sometimes it happens that way.

But you went right on living here anyway?

Yes. It's easiest to live where you have an understanding.

Death? You understand death?

No. It's more about anger. About blame.

Well, it's a very moving story.

Yes. Well, I have to go. Good luck to you.

You know, I came up here to do a story about these drownings. Now I think I might write it up with another point of view, a different slant.

Yes. Yes, that might be good.

THE SALMON

There is never, he reflected, a moment of certainty, only the illusion. And as he worked among the rocks in the middle of the river he thought on this deeply, so deeply that had his movements not been automatic he would have fallen off the rocks and into the river and been borne away.

In the summer light, even with the coolness of the water welling up around him in the air, thinking was all he was capable of; and this distraction left him exhausted and unbalanced so that at the end of the day the physical exhaustion he felt was something he lowered himself into, as into a hot bath. He pondered gentleness often. And he tried to pry (hefting the stones, conscious of the resonance between the idea in his mind and the work of his hands) into mysteries which remained as implacable as the faces of the stones.

The work was easier in the summer; in winter he was afraid of floods. He was always damp, and he slipped more often on the rocks then. In winter, on the worst days, he lost track of himself, and his acts seemed ludicrous. In summer he would feel sunlight against his back as he bent crane-like to the glacial outwash, and he enjoyed the way the light warmed his latissimi dorsi; and when the wind blew so the light seemed to have weight, he imagined how he fit into the wind, as neatly as trout poised in a deep riffle.

His hands moved over the stones (over granite, mottled

gabbro and red loaves of basalt) with a predatory finesse, flicking to rocks his eye had only that moment left, grasping, throwing in motions as smooth as his bare back under the light. He seemed as sure of himself as a cougar in ambush.

Some things he was certain of: that anadromous fish return from the ocean to spawn; that he could lift a hundred-pound rock; that it was always cooler in the evening.

At night he would sit on the porch and stare for hours at the piles of his stones, and imagine from the skeleton of the idea how he would proceed. There were technical problems, matters of physics. There were aesthetic difficulties to overcome, principally of color and texture in the materials he had to work with, but also the texture and colors, some seasonal, of the trees—maple, ash, cedar, alder, and cottonwood—on the far bank which formed a backdrop. There were anatomical details to be mindful of, a problem not only of accuracy but of verisimilitude which he felt must go to the heart of the act. He would solve each in its turn.

Out of each evening of thought he derived the energy to continue, to rise the next morning and, remembering all he had considered, to go to work, for it was (he had been told) an act of madness, and he wished above all to be sensible.

The gravel bar lay like a fish in the river, headed upstream, dark dorsal surface to the sun. Sticks of driftwood neatly enfolded on its center crest, like the collapsed spines of a fin, the dark rocks looking like scales—about it an unphraseable mood of impermanence born of its daily alteration and of eternal waiting, of migratory fish and resident stones.

He had cleared the driftwood away. He had built a bulwark

of timbers on the upstream end of the bar to divert the force of high water until he was finished, the one practical concession he had made, anchored it in the river bed, into bedrock. And there were the steel rods welded into a lattice against which he worked. The stones he fitted as haphazardly as rip-rap except on the surface, where they were fitted to bind against each other, to hold a curve in two planes without mortar. From upriver and downriver (this, in itself, two years of work) he had gathered the stones and (another year) sorted them: green shales and yellow sandstones, red slates and shaded gray gneiss, blue azurite, purple quartzes and cloudy white calcites. For iridescence, for translucence, he had to rely on individual stones and pebbles, agates, jaspers, and opals, some of which he had carried from as far away as the river's mouth.

Because his brothers had found favor with his father and he had found none, he thought. As simple as that. And a wife who had gone crazy (the fish enter the river) not out of anything he'd done or she'd done but out of the weight of her family (and move upstream), out of their perversity and sourness, generations of mistakes in which she had been a sudden clear expression, for which they had hated her. They had been afraid to have children. She was now with her sister (come upstream), reabsorbed like spent oxygen in a calm beyond his reach, forgotten but for the ingot of her that lay in him. He believed in reciprocation (come upstream) and rebalance, that others suffered as grievously as he had. He was without calculation (to spawn) or guile. And obsessed.

One evening, mired in the swamp of his thought, he leaned against the steel framework in a moment of quivering trust, as if he would weep, out of a nameless despair, and he heard coming up through the steel bars, up out of the bedrock, the murmuring of the earth—and he saw a flight of mergansers going downriver like a sigh, smelled sunshine on a thousand stones, knew by looking how cold the water would be against his belly, and that he was near the heart of it.

The room where he slept was bare as a room in a deserted hotel, but did not seem empty to him, only spare and ordered. A single shelf of books, most on the natural history of the salmonids, and a diminutive writing table, its legs barely enough to support his work (he would muse) but enough. Here some evenings, but only when he felt calm (if he was disturbed it was agony), he would write about the difficulties with his father, and of the things that had fallen apart in his life like a chrysalis flaking in a wind. He would write until he found a point of balance—and then abandon the journal as though leaping from a small airplane. On other evenings he would write in a more orderly hand and at tremendous length, sometimes until dawn: on salmon, on the dependability of their migration from the sea, on the irrefutable evidence of it. In the years until now, during the worst times, he held this idea like a walnut in his fist, cherishing its permanence, its meaning. It is how he came to conceive the stone fish.

The winter of the fourth year it began to take a finished look. He worked through these cold months and into the spring at a measured pace, which gave daily evidence of progress in spite of the enormity of the task, and also had a salutary effect on his mind. He thought less of the accidents in his life, nothing (he reflected) more than the turning of the earth, and focused instead on the sacred order to which the salmon coming upstream to spawn and die was central.

The fish was sixteen paces in length, nine feet high at the dorsal fin, *Oncorhynchus nerka*, a male sockeye with the irregularities of rut—the hooked jaw, the bright red mantel—with the air of a sumo wrestler, as Japanese in color, in its singular purpose, as a Samurai. Balanced on its belly and with its caudal fin swept to one side it was caught poised in an explosive movement. The natural armorial form of its scales served to conceal much of the stonework, but he had been so careful in the choice of stones that success here had been almost inevitable. The unsettling reality, the feeling of life in it, was heightened by the perfect shading of color, the smooth, rain-slick flanks, and the fish's eyes of hand-polished lapis, the barely visible teeth of white quartz and the narrow view down a cavernous, dark throat.

In mid-September the salmon entered the mouth of the river, two hundred miles below, and by early October they were upon him, thousands of thousands of fish, so many that they forced each other out onto the banks where the river narrowed. The movement was frantic, primal. Each year he'd watched them come finally into the small feeder creeks where, with gaping wounds washed a cloudy white, they would lie on their sides to keep one gill submerged and so breathe, move on to a pool, spawn, spill their eggs in a tail-dug basin over which the males, gaunt with hunger, glassy-eyed, exploded their milt, the seminal discharge settling over the eggs like cirrus clouds. In a matter of days they died, from which detritus their children fed. It all left him stunned.

In this year it was no different. In mid-September, into water blue-green with the mineral drainage of glaciers, the salmon who had come down this same river as small fry bore off, headed up into its reaches again. They heaved through white water where a creek washed in, some turning off, each as keen of nose as it had to be. They ate nothing, hurled themselves off the river floor into the roar of falls and rapids where they were maimed and killed and some went over and continued, dreaming perhaps of the ocean fastness and of gentler currents.

In these final months he finished. What he had imagined over the years of evenings had been engineered and it stood before him as the thing he most trusted. In the days of waiting for the salmon, he achieved a level of serenity heightened beyond any he had known before. Under this calming influence he decided impulsively to study Japanese. The connection between the fish and the culture seemed to him both incongruous and appropriate. He could imagine salmon choosing to live in Japanese houses, which had about them something of the ocean, which seemed submerged. He could think of the fish writing in that apposite calligraphy, that if they left messages they would leave them in this form, and on rice tissue papers as delicate and strong as the walls of the house.

One evening in October when he had begun to worry that the fish would not come, a rain storm swept up the valley. The great stone fish glistened as though it had just at that moment burst forth. Walking out to it, he felt a fierce pride in its form, and he headed downriver with this idea. In the shallows after a few hundred yards—it was difficult to see but the rain-shattered surface of the river revealed it with a precision that startled him—were salmon, their dark glistening backs as far as he could see. For several moments it was not clear to him what they were doing, that they were slowly turning around. The rain, sweep-

64

ing in wind-driven sheets, made a sound that sheltered him from panic, but his guts fell away from his heart. He turned to look upstream at the stone fish, one lapis eye glaring with its black shining obsidian pupil in the turned head, the jaw agape, and the monument struck him suddenly with the depth of his desperation—the pages of his journal, the words pounded out like this rain on his shoulders. Overwhelmed with an understanding of the assumption in his act, made the more grotesque by its perfection, he waded stupified into the water where the fish maneuvered, milling, trying to turn around. He staggered amongst them, trying to form a statement of apology, putting his fingers to their dark backs until they were gone, until he realized that they were gone.

He brought his hands to his face and for a while, in the passing mist of the rainstorm, he imagined what they would say. That it was the presence of the stone fish that had offended them (he tried to grasp the irreverence of it, how hopelessly presumptuous it must have seemed), that it was an order born out of fear, understood even by salmon, to be discarded as quickly as nightmares so that life could go on.

When he stood beside the fish he realized for the first time how flawless it was, that the ravages of the upstream journey were nowhere revealed. He thought of dismantling it, but instead removed only the obsidian pupils from the lapis eyes, which he dropped without looking into the rushing water as he crossed to the opposite bank.

In later years he wrote poetry in a beautiful Japanese hand in which he balanced the stonework of Machu Picchu against the directionless flight of butterflies. In this manner he slowly reclaimed his own life.

HANNER'S
STORY

There are those who say that things were once better in this valley, that many years ago there was a different kind of life. I have listened patiently to these stories. They are idyllic and farfetched. I believe they represent hopeful longing on the part of those who tell them, a wish for a more orderly life, a life, ultimately, less cruel to them. These stories—they are called Sheffield stories—are told principally by the older people, the life-long residents, and evangelically, as though to overcome and smother incipient suspicion in the listener. I go on listening, though there seems no chance now that they will supply the detail I wish to hear, because of the attitude they have taken.

There is a man called Hanner, a retired guide on the river, who worked in his youth in the woods (as have most men here), whose hands bear the marks of trouble with wire rope and fish line and knives, who appears to have given his life over to a trenchant bitterness. The roots of it may be older, but he has been visited late in life by every tragedy. His only son went to prison for a criminal act with a child. His wife died of leukemia, slowly and before he retired. Vandals have smashed the windshield of his pickup on different occasions and turned his horses loose. One of the horses, a roan mare he never rode, was struck and killed by a school bus. He is without family. He does little in a day but move from one cafe to another drinking coffee and listening in silence to the stories around him. Sometimes he tells stories, about fishing. About outlanders he has guided down the river. People consider him sour, self-absorbed, and without wisdom. But he has lived here all his life and they say he is sharp-eyed; and that cannot be overlooked by someone like myself, they have said, interested in verifying a story.

Hearing all this, I would think to myself: he will not lie.

When I first encountered Hanner he was standing at a distance with his hands in the pockets of his khaki trousers, silhouetted in the tunnel of his open barn against a pale blue summer sky. I needed directions, and in search of local knowledge had wandered much farther onto his property than I wished. He seemed to be doing nothing at all; with a sideward movement of his head he gave me his attention as I approached. He was detached though explicit in giving directions and I went on to find my way without trouble.

I walked away from the barn that day constricted in the throat, believing that for all the disparagement Hanner gripped something remote and wild.

The next time we met I had occasion to pick him up along the road. He would not have solicited a ride; his pickup was out of service (I had seen it in town, at the station) and as I saw him walking with a large brown bag in his arms and slowed I recognized him and offered him a ride. I dropped him off. He was cordial but did not invite me to dinner. The third time I saw him was in the evening. He was standing alone in the middle of a one-lane logging bridge looking down at the river. I do not, again, know what he was doing. Perhaps he contemplated suicide. I stopped part way onto the bridge. He turned; we regarded each other. It was clear I was intruding, but as I moved off he stayed me with his raised hands and said he would walk back with me. I wondered that someone else had my habit of walking in the dark, but asked him instead about the stories.

He sighed, as though caught in a great undertow, an obligation that meant a diversion from his purposes. But an obligation. His circumspect nature, I thought, would work in his favor as an arbiter of detail in such dreams as I had been hearing—if one indeed were interested in what had happened, as, to an extent, I was.

It was rubbish he told me, those stories of Sheffield. Told by disillusioned people (I raised my eyebrows in the darkness) who wanted to be more than they actually were, or to wound. He, himself, was bitter over events in his own life but (I could feel him shaking his head as we moved along the edge of the road beneath the trees) he did not delude himself. He lived within the moment of his life, harsh as it was, and blamed no one. He saw nothing but pining weakness in the Sheffield stories. They left you empty, he said, when you heard them, because they were full of a kind of hope that insulted life. They were disrespectful, he said.

The central history, from which the stories derive, is short. In 1841 an Illinois man called William Alder came into the valley and established a secular community like the one at New Harmony. The community was named Sheffield after the first family to have a child, a girl named Wilhelmina, and it prospered, due principally to a fortuitous location. There was rich alluvial soil in the river's floodplain, and there were open meadows between oak and ash islands in which to build and plant without the necessity of clearing timber. The hunting was good, the winter weather rainy but mild. (It was here, in sketching for me the original beauty of the area, that I heard the greatest embroidery and a wonderment in the voices.) But their fortune was still greater. On their very first visit to the ocean, only seventy miles farther west, they found a shipwreck, its hull intact and most of its stores dry and undisturbed. There was rock salt, copper sheathing, iron implements, calico cloth—it is hard to be sure what, precisely, was found, but they returned to the valley with all of it in several trips in one of the ship's lifeboats, in itself a good find.

There was a third factor that must be considered in the success of the community and though it is rarely emphasized it seems to me to be the most important. It had to do with the community's reception by the Quotaka, the native people of the region. They were a tall, Athabascan-speaking group described in the journals of Robert Gray, Donald McKenzie, and other early visitors as exceedingly hostile and treacherous. Among the Quotaka was a medicine man called Elishtanak. Incredibly, he was the physical twin in every aspect of William Alder. It seems the Quotaka must have looked on this favorably for they seemed to have indulged the settlers' presence immediately. It could just as well have been disastrous; they might have considered the uncanny resemblance blasphemous and killed every one of them. As it was, the Sheffield group and the Quotaka remained close. There were one or two intermarriages, though it seems no other formal bonds were ever avowed. (I am relying here principally on William Alder's journal.) After these initial years of cooperative alliance, the Quotaka succumbed completely to a smallpox epidemic that left the Sheffield community relatively unscathed.

It is this early, idyllic period of mutualism between about

1843 and 1847 or 48 that most often serves as an epiphany in the stories I have heard. There are no denouements. What is there at the end is rapture in the face of the teller; an earnest, inquisitive look directed at the listener and a kind of wistfulness I find discomforting.

The story would often seem no more to the teller than an extraordinary history which spoke well of the natural attributes of the country and was naively instructional in the Christian virtues, though one hesitated to be cynical. The various embellishments emphasized, beyond the beauty of the region, ingenuous sharing and cooperation, an absence of violence and a good relationship with the Quotaka. It is with this that I gradually grew a little impatient, believing the thread of something important had been lost. Even more distracting to me was that among all the episodes there were so few that bore on the Quotaka, or indeed on the profound and central enigma of Sheffield: one afternoon in 1857 an itinerant tinsmith found the community deserted. No note of explanation. Signs of local flooding but no other sign of hardship. No one in the community was ever seen again.

In spite of these difficulties I was from the beginning taken with these stories, which could be heard in the cafes and taverns or over dinner in peoples' homes, to which I was occasionally invited. I confirmed some of the particulars in libraries and archives. It seemed, from Alder's journal, which he kept through 1854, and other documents of the time, that the community did uncommonly well. But it also came to an end, and no one I spoke with wanted to talk about that, or even considered it important. They only enjoyed the first part of the story.

The evening Hanner and I walked down the road together

he told me he thought the Sheffield community had eventually failed, as all such idealistic groups do; that they were as contentious as any group, as taken with a sense of cultural primacy and, ultimately, personal need. The Quotaka interested him more. A Quotaka, he said, had taught him how to fish.

We walked on in silence. It was on my mind to quiz Hanner closely on certain points when he began abruptly to speak.

"The man's name was Elishtanak. When my father died he came and asked my mother if he could take me fishing, and he made a regular thing of it. He understood fishing, and that's what he taught me, to understand the obligations and the mutual courtesies involved. He would sit on the bank of the river with me and talk about steelhead and chinook as well as anyone who ever wrote it down. I've fished this river the way he taught me and fished it better than anyone. And every day I did it the feeling filled me that I was sure of myself, that because I understood this I could weather anything.

"Elishtanak told me a story. One time" (Hanner's voice changed in such a way that the hair went up on the back of my neck and I leaned forward involuntarily, as though about to be overtaken by something in the dark) "before there were any people walking around this valley there were bear people. They had an agreement with the salmon." Hanner put his fingers to his forehead, as though coming into a memory of it. "The salmon would come upriver every fall and the bears would acknowledge this and take what they needed. This is the way it was with everything. Everyone lived by certain agreements and courtesies. But the salmon people and the bear people had made no agreement with the river. It had been overlooked. No one thought it was even necessary. Well, it was. One fall the river

74

pulled itself back into the shore trees and wouldn't let the salmon enter from the ocean. Whenever they would try, the river would pull back and leave the salmon stranded on the beach. There was a long argument, a lot of talk. Finally the river let the salmon enter. But when the salmon got up into this country where the bears lived the river began to run in two directions at once, north on one side, south on the other, roaring, heaving, white water, and rolling big boulders up on the banks. Then the river was suddenly still. The salmon were afraid to move. The bears were standing behind trees, looking out. The river said in the middle of all this silence that there had to be an agreement. No one could just do something, whatever they wanted. You couldn't just take someone for granted.

"So for several days they spoke about it. The salmon said who they were and where they came from, and the bears spoke about what they did, what powers they had been given, and the river spoke about its agreement with the rain and the wind and the crayfish and so on. Everybody said what they needed and what they would give away. Then a very odd thing happened—the river said it loved the salmon. No one had ever said anything like this before. No one had taken this chance. It was an honesty that pleased everyone. It made for a very deep agreement among them.

"Well they were able to reach an understanding about their obligations to each other and everyone went his way. This remains unchanged. Time has nothing to do with this. This is not a story. When you feel the river shuddering against your legs, you are feeling the presence of all these agreements."

We walked on.

"I think those people at Sheffield just went their separate

ways, but maybe they never made an agreement with the river, and the Quotaka hated them so much for it that after the epidemic they never told them you had to do that, and that's what happened. A flood. Quick, in the middle of the night, into their homes. I don't know. You can feel the anger in water behind a dam."

I sensed, off to my left, the moonlit running of the river, heard its muffled voice. We continued down the road, abandoned at this late hour by cars. Hanner looked off into the darkness and I felt an insect land suddenly in my ear.

DAWN

Apricots. It was because the water smelled like apricots as much as anything that she went down to the water. She rose in the darkness and dressed and went down through the trees, trailing her fingers, touching plants she knew but whose names she'd never taken to mind—*syringa*, someone once said, for the mock orange, whose leaves reminded her of silk. *Silkbush*. Rhododendron. Leather-leaved and masculine. Huckleberry. Small leaves stiff with fear. Drops of water from a midnight shower perched on each leaf, resting on the earth grass and broken under her bare feet walking. Mist against her face. Female rain. (Rain in sheets hammering the river, *chuuuuuuush* all afternoon, flattening the riffles, stretching the skin of surface water taut. Male rain.)

She would rise and dress and go down through the trees to the rocks and sit, gather her knees against her chest and smell the metal odor of the water (feel how her pelvis worked against the rock, and the cool wetness of her feet with the dew [female rain] on them and she imagined how wide her eyes must be in the dark), an odor which would change with the light.

Around her in the water, because they could not be seen, had nothing to fear, male mergansers—red feather, blue feather, yellow feather, brown, white feather, white feather, iridescent green—and female mergansers—gray blue, gray blue gray blue gray blue warrior feather gray blue (twenty-one with her, against the osprey) and a little maroon. Slept. Ducks slept. Beneath them salmon slept. Beneath them the river undulated, like sun-dried bed linen shaken out in a French hotel room in the countryside.

While she dreamed of English museums (he wanted to go on, always, to some other thing), of how to ask a question, a weasel slipped onto the dark rock, quivering, nose in the air, neck rammed out stiff. She heard the crockery sound of water as it flowed around the rocks and it made her sympathetic. The weasel shot to her, stopped short, saw the size of her against the stars and ran.

Europe, she thought, seeing the way someone ate torte, remembering her fingers on Laocoön's marble calf in the Vatican, smelling cappuccino, came on a schedule not hers.

She would come down to the river in the morning naked under the print dress bought on the road to somewhere (New Mexico: he would know) because she wanted to cover herself, be covered by this dress, this loose, fitting loosely this way, and the print of fleur-de-lis, something small, blue against the off-white exactly. Cotton. This exactly. Ten dollars. Yes, exactly this. He didn't like it.

She would go down in the morning through the trees, touch the leaves of plants whose names she did not know, naked under the print dress, female rain on the bridge of her nose.

Above her head (she thought of the female merganser poised on the rock mid-river, the ducklings around her, the osprey hidden in shadow high in the cottonwood) in the limbs of an ash tree a gray owl was taking a weasel apart. In the east the black was a deeper blue, the color of the days around her father's death. Exactly. And got bluer and the water, the river, became visible and black. She stretched her legs out, matching her calves and arching her feet, the unfolding beginning there, and with her palms flat on the rock and her head lolling backward she lifted her chest until her spine bent like a bow, shuddered (remembering the osprey motionless in the shadows, watching the merganser and the ducklings huddled on the rock knowing [he had explained all this later] as long as they stayed on the rock, covering it as they did, he would not stoop). And up in the house he rolled over and did not sense that she was gone.

She would go down to the river while it was still dark, and know by the call of the thrushes when it was light enough (opening her eyes, having been at the memory of some cheese like Gouda but with another name in a village [Lyons?] and how he had looked away as though embarrassed when she said sexual, how sexual)—light enough to see the path through the trees. But she went when she went always before dawn, before she could see.

One morning in the gray light, its sound at first submerged in the river's movements, a dory came. A man in a hat rowing. Moving downriver, as foreign as anything she could imagine. Another stood in the bow. He wore another hat and was dressed in neat khaki clothing. She saw the gentle whip of his fly rod pointing into the slack water behind large rocks, after rainbow trout. He looked—exactly the word she was after—silly. But he whipped the rod to set the fly here and there, time and again, the other man rowing, now the rattle of an oarlock, the boat moving toward her, the excessive neatness of their clothing, the creases, the grim expression clear on their red, razor-stropped faces, rowing hard. She froze with the weight of lead in her belly, coming that fast across the water toward her—never saw her, whipping the shallows for fish, went by, thirty feet away. Silly. Her face quivered. Silly. She put her hands, her palms cold from the rock, against her face.

Winter and summer she would come down to be in the rocks by the water, lying in the dark, waiting for the light, as though by the act itself she could overcome her losses. She meant to remember to tell someone—how the colors came out each morning, how she would like *layers of fabric like this*, a dress where the wind blew each layer open, somehow. In the beginning only the blue blacks, very cool, all the way through to the red of a certain beetle brilliant on her kneecap at ten o'clock, to white Caribbean pastels at noon. Somehow.

She would undress and with sprinkling sounds wash her hands and her face (the osprey, giving up, lifted off the cottonwood limb and flew on upriver, and the merganser, when he was gone, led the ducklings off the rock—twenty-one, she counted them [he said no, that the book said fourteen, tops]—across open water to the protection of overhanging trees along the bank. Had waited him out, staring down at her from the tree, had kept them all still on the rock, never mentioning the osprey, telling a story, telling many stories until he went upriver and she could lead them to the protection of trees along the bank) and slip naked into the water, her orifices closing against the coolness, her skin tightening. The current was too strong and there were too many rocks, clearly visible now, green with moss and stones to bruise her knees in the shallows. She went out from the rock, caught the surge around it and went downstream to a place where she grabbed maple branches and swung around on her belly to face the current. The water lifted her up and when she spread her legs let her down. She closed her eyes and let the water break around her nose and lifted, against her breasts, arched her back, the current against her hips, opened her legs and sank down. She imagined herself among salmon (against her, opened her legs and sank down), swimming gently among salmon (lifting, sank down), until the light seemed much brighter, birds quieter, and she was wide-eyed, afraid of being seen, that the privacy of her morning had broken like an eggshell, and she came out on the bank.

She sat down on the rock in the print dress, the sunlight prickling with the coolness of the river over her and feeling the movement of air over the rock. She dried her eyes with the hem of the dress and saw in the island of hair between her legs suspended—she was overcome with tenderness—two small bits of alder leaf, bright green.

She sat there, damp in the dress, feeling taut in a way that pleased her. She thought of him asleep up there in the house, of how the water (she had told him and he had smiled) at this time in the morning smelled like apricots. Exactly.

UPRIVER

The course of the river above the falls is largely unknown, for the climb is arduous and at that point the road passes near and provides a view to satisfy most. The country on up to the headwaters has been walked by government men looking for clues to mineral deposits and to complete maps, but it remains unknown nevertheless. The illusion has been sustained, if one asks around or consults a topographic map, that it is well known; but I know this to be false. And I cannot help but marvel at how little care has been taken in making certain distinctions. For example, at the headwaters itself, farther up than is shown, ravens are meditating, and it is from *them* that the river actually flows, for at night they break down and weep; the universal anguish of creatures, their wailing in desolation, the wrenching anger of betrayals—this seizes them and passes out of them and in that weeping the river takes its shape.

Any act of kindness of which they hear, no matter how filled with trepidation, brings up a single tear, and it, too, runs down the black bills, splashes on small stones and is absorbed in the trickle. Farther along the murmur of fish enters, and the sensation of your hands on sheets of cold steel, the impenetrable wall presented by certain deep shades of blue, the sound of a crack working its way through a plate of English china; this sound, the sound of quick drawn breath, the odor of humus, an image of the earth hurtling through space with thought ripped from its surface, left floating like shredded fabric in its wake, the loss of what is imagined but uncared for—all this is wound among the tears of bending pain and moments of complete vulnerability in each of us to form, finally, visible water, and farther on a creek, limpid and cool, of measurable dimension.

I have in the past recounted these observations to audiences poorly chosen and have had to move on after the silent reception, a narrow-eyed, malevolent squinting behind me, as though I were waking to knowledge of a cobra in a dark room. But this does not disturb me. The images are irrefutable, requiring only patience to perceive. They come into view as easily as a book is hooked with a finger and pulled from a shelf. But perhaps you already know this.

In recent years I have spent considerable time above the falls, along what I believe to be an unknown section of the river. It is in some ways the most dangerous country, reverberating with hope, seducing in its simplicity. It is little traveled. I mean to examine things slowly and thoroughly there; as often as I have failed at it, gone running with gleeful intuition toward what seemed an answer, I have hauled myself back, returned again to a strict and ordered course. After the initial, difficult survey I began to examine short sections of the river one at a time in the hope—beguiling but achingly real—of a larger vision. I noted, therefore, which creatures frequented each portion of the bank, the kind and number of riparian plants, the shape and structure of pebbles, the time of breezes, as well as the small and easily missed traces of observations not my own. I strove to be complete in my examinations, yet to not lean toward arrogance or presumption. In this way I came to a bend in the river one day from which I could see a house, which I slowly approached.

It was painted gray, with deep blue shutters in the Cape Cod style. Four stories pitched against the side of a steep hill, the windows casement-hung with small panes of leaded glass. A broad porch, on which moved the teasing shadows of tree limbs. My hand took the white porcelain doorknob of a French door. Its glass tempered the light, as I closed it behind me, to the interior of the house. The floors were oak parquet, the rooms spacious with centered rugs of Indonesian hemp, as thick underfoot as moss. The walls were papered in such a way as to appear distant, ghostly, as though seen underwater; at times the light interrupted them altogether. They were—one of the things one remembers for no reason, with which one insulates himself against all that is unknown—Cockerell marbled papers, from England, elegantly designed and of those colors between primary and pastel that burst on you like a forgotten name or the taste of a peach.

The furniture consisted of a few pieces, thoughtfully placed. A chair or two, often set alone by a window, as though someone had been watching, had just stepped into another room, was listening now in a stillness that suggested canyons or regret. A woman's bed, with a brass bedstead and a spread of soft chenille, white as sun-bleached seashells, on which, somehow, light was always falling and on which she and I would lie, trusting, and fall asleep in the afternoon.

In one or two of the rooms were tables, of the sort one might choose to sit alone at to write a letter. I would sit and watch the river move through the trees, my hands folded on the table or cupped in my lap, with a look (she would say) of dismay and acceptance.

We would dance. We would remove our shoes and with only that slight chirp of skin against the oak floor we would dance to an imagined music until we were brought around by a movement of wind through the house and in our ecstasy another rhythm: songs remembered from springs of celebration in country close by, where the oaks grew once, implacable, hosting sparrows, rising now out of the floor as though released again. In moments of vulnerability such as this we would not speak and hardly move. Strands of her hair stuck to my cheek, the sound of our breathing. Out of respect for the floor.

The trees outside barely moved, thoughts passing sub rosa leaf to leaf.

In a room I entered for the first time one fall I found a book. It was left open on the window sill, as though someone would return. It was printed in a language I do not know which I nevertheless read, page by page, as though sensing a promise in the very form of the words and sentences and the feel of the chapter breaks of imminent revelation. None was forthcoming and I abandoned this project.

We danced, most often. And in the evening I would tell stories. The way we desired each other became dance and stories, and the passion took us as deeply, left us embracing and protective.

In that time I do not remember ever being away, though I know I was. Even now in the memory of it I do not know where I am. I know that I still spend time in the upper part of the river and that those relationships I hold to be true, such as that between anguish and the birth of rivers, endure.

Farther up the river are the unfolding of other relationships, together with the loss of the promise of anything to be found. I have been led to believe that that is the reason no one goes up that far, though the promise, in its way, is kept. It is the walk home that is terrifying.

DROUGHT

I awoke one night and thought I heard rain—it was the dry needles of fir trees falling on the roof. Men with an intolerable air of condolence have appeared, as though drawn by the smell of death, dressed comfortably, speaking a manipulated tongue, terminally evil. They have inquired into the purchase of our homes. And reporters come and go, outraged over the absence of brown trout, which have never been here. The river like some great whale lies dying in the forest.

In the years we have been here I have trained myself to listen to the river, not in the belief that I could understand what it said, but only from one day to the next know its fate. The river's language arose principally from two facts: the slightest change in its depth brought it into contact with a different portion of the stones along its edges and the rocks and boulders mid-stream that lay in its way, and so changed its tone; and although its movement around one object may seem uniform at any one time it is in fact changeable. Added to these major variations are the landings of innumerable insects on its surface, the breaking of its waters by fish, the falling into it of leaves and twigs, the slooshing of raccoons, the footfalls of deer; ultimately these are only commentary on the river's endless reading of the surface of the earth over which it flows.

It was in this way that I learned before anyone else of the coming drought. Day after day as the river fell by imperceptible increments its song changed, notes came that were unknown to me. I mentioned this to no one, but each morning when I awoke I went immediately to the river's edge and listened. It was as though I could hear the sound rain begins to make in a country where it is not going to come for a long time.

As the water fell, however, nothing unexpected was uncovered, although the effect of standing in areas once buried beneath the roar of the river's current was unsettling. I found only one made object, a wheel, the kind you find on the back of a child's tricycle. But I didn't look as closely as the others. The wailing of the river over its last stones was difficult to bear, yet it was this that drew me back each day, as one visits those dying hopelessly in a hospital room. During those few hours each morning I would catch stranded fish barehanded in shallow pools and release them where the river still flowed. The bleaching of algae once waving green underwater to white; river stones once cool now hot to the touch and dry; spider webs stretched where there had been salmon eggs; snakes where there had been trout—it was as though the river had been abandoned.

During those summer days, absorbed with the death of the river and irritated at the irreverent humor of weather forecasters in distant cities, I retreated into a state of isolation. I fasted and abstained as much as I felt appropriate from water. These were only gestures, of course, but even as a boy I knew a gesture might mean life or death and I believed the universe was similarly triggered.

From this point on, the song that came out of the river did not bother me as much. I sat out of the way of the pounding sun, in dark rocks shaded by the overhanging branches of alders along the bank. Their dry leaves, stirred by the breeze, fell brittle and pale around me. I slept on the bank regularly now. I would say very simple prayers in the evening, only an expression of camaraderie, stretching my fingers gently into the darkness toward the inchoate source of the river's strangulation. I did not beg. There was a power to dying, and it should be done with grace. I was only making a gesture on the shore, a speck in the steep, brutal dryness of the valley by a dying river.

In moments of great depression, of an unfathomable compassion in myself, I would make the agonized and tentative movements of a dance, like a long-legged bird. I would exhort the river.

What death we saw. Garter snake stiff as a twig in the rocks. Trees (young ones, too young) crying out in the night, shuddering, dropping all their leaves. Farther from the river, birds falling dead in thickets, animals dead on the paths, their hands stiffened in gestures of bewilderment and beseeching; the color gone out of the eyes of any creature you met, for whom, out of respect, you would step off the path to allow to pass.

Where a trickle of water still flowed there was an atmosphere of truce, more dangerous than one might imagine. As deer and coyote sipped from the same tiny pool they abrogated their agreement, and the deer contemplated the loss of the coyote as he would the loss of a friend; for the enemy, like the friend, made you strong. I was alert for such moments, for they were augury, but I was as wary of them as of any lesson learned in death.

One moonlit evening I dreamed of a certain fish. The fish was gray-green against light-colored stones at the bottom of a deep pool, breathing a slow, unperturbed breathing, the largest fish I had ever imagined living in the river. The sparkling of the water around him and the sound of it cascading over the creek bed made me weak and I awoke suddenly, convulsed. I knew the fish. I knew the place. I set out immediately.

The dry riverbed was only a clatter of teetering stones now, ricocheting off my feet as I passed, bone weary, feeling disarmed by hunger, by the dimness of the night, and by the irrefutable wisdom and utter foolishness of what I was doing. As I drew near the mouth of the creek the fish began to loom larger and larger and I could feel—as though my hands were extended to a piece of cloth flapping in the darkness—both the hope and the futility of such acts.

I found the spot where the creek came in and went up it. I had seen the fish once in a deep pool below a rapids where he had fed himself too well and grown too large to escape. There was a flow of night air coming down the creek bed, rattling dry leaves. In the faint moonlight a thousand harlequin beetles suddenly settled on my clothing and I knew how close I was to a loss of conviction, to rage, to hurling what beliefs I had like a handful of pebbles into the bushes.

The beetles clung to the cloth, moved through my hair, came into the cups of my hands as I walked, and as suddenly were gone, and the area I stood in was familiar, the fish before me. The rapids were gone. The pool had become a pit. In its lowest depression the huge fish lay motionless, but for the faint lifting of a gill cover. I climbed down to him and wrapped him in my shirt, soaked in the pool. I had expected, I think, a fight, to be punched in that pit by the fish who lay in my arms now like a cold lung.

Climbing out of there, stopping wherever I could to put his head under in some miserable pool, hurrying, I came to the river and the last trickle of water, where I released him without ceremony.

I knew, as I had known in the dream, the danger I was in but I knew, too, that without such an act of self-assertion no act of humility had meaning.

By now the river was only a whisper. I stood at the indistinct edge and exhorted what lay beyond the river, which now seemed more real than the river itself. With no more strength than there is in a bundle of sticks I tried to dance, to dance the dance of the long-legged birds who lived in the shallows. I danced it because I could not think of anything more beautiful.

The turning came during the first days of winter. Lynx came down from the north to what was left of the river. Deer were with him. And from some other direction Raccoon and Porcupine. And from downriver Weasel and White-footed Mouse, and from above Blue Heron and Goshawk. Badger came up out of the ground with Mole. They stood near me in staring silence and I was afraid to move. Finally Blue Heron spoke: "We were the first people here. We gave away all the ways of living. Now no one remembers how to live anymore, so the river is drying up. Before we could ask for rain there had to be someone to do something completely selfless, with no hope of success. You went after that fish, and then at the end you were trying to dance. A person cannot be afraid of being foolish. For everything, every gesture, is sacred.

"Now, stand up and learn this dance. It is going to rain."

We danced together on the bank. And the songs we danced to were the river songs I remembered from long ago. We danced until I could not understand the words but only the sounds, and the sounds were unmistakably the sound rain makes when it is getting ready to come into a country.

I awoke in harsh light one morning, moved back into the trees and fell asleep again. I awoke later to what I thought were fir needles falling on my cheeks but these were drops of rain.

It rained for weeks. Not hard, but steadily. The river came back easily. There were no floods. People said it was a blessing. They offered explanations enough. Backs were clapped, reputations lost and made, the seeds of future argument and betrayal sown, wounds suffered and allowed, pride displayed. It was no different from any other birth but for a lack of joy and, for that, stranger than anything you can imagine, inhuman and presumptuous. But people go their way, and with reason; and the hardness for some is all but unfathomable, and so begs forgiveness. Everyone has to learn how to die, that song, that dance, alone and in time.

The river has come back to fit between its banks. To stick your hands into the river is to feel the cords that bind the earth together in one piece. The sound of it at a distance is like wild horses in a canyon, going sure-footed away from the smell of a cougar come to them faintly on the wind.

Barry Lopez's articles, essays, and fiction appear regularly in such publications as *Harper's* and *North American Review*, where he is a contributing editor. He is the author of *Of Wolves and Men* and *Desert Notes: Reflections in the Eye of a Raven*, the first book in a trilogy of fiction which includes *River Notes*. He lives near Finn Rock, Oregon.